Older than Dirt

with *Notes from an*

Old Cow Belle

by
Ina Murray

PublishAmerica
Baltimore

ISBN: 1-4241-1398-9
PUBLISHED BY PUBLISHAMERICA, LLLP
www.publishamerica.com
Baltimore

Printed in the United States of America

A Note from the Author

Many of the following poems were "born in the barn."

While Husband and I were farming, one of my jobs was carrying pails of milk from the milking machines in the barn, to the milk house, and then pour the milk through a stainless steel strainer into the huge stainless steel bulk tank.

It was then that I would hurriedly jot down a verse of two on one of the big round thirteen inch filter discs. Until I would hear Husband yell: "THE PAILS ARE FULL!!"

I dedicate this book to the memory of that dear man, known to the public as "Husband", who had patience to put up with the "Old Cow" for forty seven years, until his death in 1993.

I further dedicate it to our four children, eleven grand children, and five great-grandchildren (with more on the horizon) They make life worth living!

I pray that by reading these poems and writing, someone, somewhere, may be blessed by them, and draw closer to God because of them. Then I too, will be truly blessed, by leaving something worthwhile behind when I am gone.

With Thanks and Praise to the Lord!

Ina Murray

About the Author

Ina Murray, Ellsworth, Wisconsin, former farm wife, mother of four, grandmother of eleven, great-grandmother of five plus, writer, columnist of thirty years "Notes From An Old Cow Belle," Hospice volunteer, Guideposts Prayer Volunteer, Member of Our Savior's Lutheran Church, Beldenville, Wisconsin.

Ina lives in her little log home with her dog Bailey, at the top of the El Paso hill.

Older than Dirt
with Notes from an Old Cow Belle

I am convinced that God has a great sense of humor. We know that His Word tells us that if we remain in Him, we will continue to become more and more like him every year.

And I know He has a sense of humor. He created me, didn't he? That should be proof. But as I grow older, and try to become more like Him, I realize that my sense of humor has also become keener than in my younger years. I wonder why that is. Maybe because age brings with it a relaxation that allows humor to rule over worry, anxiety and paranoia.

I like to look back on some of the funnier events in my life, and get a second laugh from them. Like: When my grandson, Travis, was about nine years old, and still enjoyed going out to lunch with Grandma, I took him to the Red Barn for lunch one day.

After lunch, he dashed into the adjoining gift shop, saying, "I'll just be a minute, Grandma. And say, how old are you?" I told him I am over 60.

He soon returned carrying a small brown paper bag, which he gave to me, saying "I bought you a present Grandma, for taking me to lunch."

I opened the bag and took out a round colorful pin. Travis grinned as I read it, "Older Than Dirt." I laughed too, and pinned it on my jacket.

Since then, each year on my birthday, I pin that little reminder on my clothes, and it gives me a chuckle, remembering all those fun times with Travis. Travis is now twenty years old, towers over me, and takes his girl friend to lunch.

On Being a Farmer's Wife

Being a farmer's wife with all it's little irritations and frustrations, makes it absolutely necessary to have a strong, healthy sense of humor. If you don't laugh, you cry.

I was always the "gopher" for Husband. I would run all the errands, getting parts for broken machinery, or twine, if we ran out in the middle of a field of hay, or anything that would save my Husband some time. Because of course, being a mother of four, and a helper on the farm, I had more leisure time than he did.

Once when we ran out of filter discs, I was elected to "run to town" and buy some before the evening milking time. Filter discs came before the evolution of pipeline milking. Filter discs were put into a large stainless steel strainer to strain out any impurities when the milk was poured into the bulk tank.

I 'ran' to our nearby town, Ellsworth. They didn't have any discs that size, so I "ran" to the next town, Red Wing and entered the F and D Store. To save time, I asked the clerk where I would find 13 inch filter discs. She told me to go down the aisle, turn the corner, and ask the young man to show you.

I did, but there weren't any. The young boy said they were out of that size. So I hurried back up the aisle, and on the way I spotted a tub of men's work sox. The tan kind with the white toes and heels. They were on sale, so I grabbed a bundle, hustled up to the check out, and placing them on the counter, I commented "Funny filter discs, huh? Do you think they'll work?"

The clerk looked at me like I was mad, and sputtered, "Well, well, I don't know how." Then shrugging her shoulders she said, "Well, it's your money. Do what you want with it."

I didn't tell her any difference, but I did chuckle all the way out to the pickup.

* * *

As we speak of filter discs, I must mention that those round, white pieces of whatever they were made of, are where a lot of my writings and poems began. So, many of the things I've written have been born in the barn.

Back when we were hard at farming, before we had much of any conveniences, I was the person who carried the milk from the barn into the milk house in two tall pails. Then I would dump the milk into the strainers, and go back and set them in front of whatever cow Husband was milking.

Then I would dash back into the milk house and jot down a few more lines of a poem, sometimes getting lost in it, until I would hear a roar from the inner sanctum, "THE PAILS ARE FULL!!" Then, leaving off my scribbling, I would dash back into the barn for two more pails of milk. Husband had a lot of patience to put up with that for so many years.

* * *

This book, "Older Than Dirt" is derived from the weekly column I have written since 1976. The very first one reveals how much patience Husband needed to stay married to me. This column was written in 1976, but lived in my desk drawer for six years, until I finally had courage enough to submit it to the Country Edition of the Red Wing Republican Eagle, where it stayed for several years.

When that supplement was discontinued, I brought a few samples to the Pierce County Herald's then editor, Jay Griggs. The column is called Notes From an Old Cow Belle, and that cow has remained in that pasture all these years, now with Bill Kirk as editor, and is still grazing there.

That first column went like this:

NOTES FROM AN OLD COW BELLE

How I envy those organized women, who do not deviate from their household chores; but go from task to task, and in the middle of the forenoon, can sit down in a spic and span house to enjoy a cup of coffee!

My intentions are so good, but I am so easily distracted. Just walking the few yards from the barn to the house, I can use up an hour or two, waddling around on my haunches, examining small smooth stones, "just right for lady bugs and bluebirds."

Then, when I finally get in the house, I Must wash them and dry them to have them ready to paint on. And then, those smooth surfaces are too tempting, and out come the paints.

All too soon, about 11:30, dear, patient Husband comes in and asks, "Aren't we having any lunch today?"

So, talking fast, laughing a lot, I hastily clear away the breakfast dishes (yes, they are still sitting there, unwashed), cheerily suggesting grilled cheese sandwiches and promising roast beef for supper.

Some of the biggest changes since that time, are: I no longer waddle around on my haunches. I can't even crouch like that. If I tried I would fall flat on my face or tip over backwards. I still waddle, but I do it standing up.

Another change is that I certainly don't paint lady bugs any more. They remind me too much of the Asian beetles that have invaded my house these past couple of years.

If you are wondering about the bluebirds and lady bugs, they used to be a part of the huge "Welcome" rocks I made. They had to be pretty big, able to stand erect, and have one flat side for painting the message. Like "WELCOME TO THE ANDERSONS" or whatever the order wanted. I would paint shamrocks, or flowers or sometimes a flag; and then glue on a little painted bluebird or lady bug on the top. Then the whole thing would be coated with polyurethane to keep it from weathering.

I actually used to drive out into farmers; fields to their rock piles (with their permission) to find these monstrous rocks. I would load them onto the tail gate of the pickup, take them home and clean them off and paint them. That's how I ruined my wrists and my dining room table. Fool.

Recently I learned that those welcome rocks lasted a long time. A woman mentioned to me that she still had hers after 25 years and it turned out to have an unusual purpose. Her house was broken into one night, and the culprits had thrown that welcome rock through the window to gain entrance. Who would ever have thought?

* * *

Another creation of mine that began on a white filter disc, is the poem "Limitations." Born from an everlasting feeling in inadequacy, this seems to say it all.
Realizing how limited I am in attaining so many things, and the wonder of all the things God has made, for our enjoyment, the words of this poem just flowed out onto the white filter disc, verse by verse.

In my crude attempts to praise the Lord for His goodness, and to share the wonder of His Son's sacrifice for us all, most of the things I write 'need' to proclaim Him. In the poem, Limitations, one verse is significant in this. It says " I cannot measure up to that, which God would have me be; but I can shout about His love. He gave His Son for me!"

That poem has been published and copied, made into decorative plaques and set to music. But....since I didn't copyright it, it was also abused.

A Hardware Company asked permission to use it in their Christmas Publication, and I agreed. But when I got the copy of the publication, they had taken the liberty of omitting that 'key' verse, and so the whole meaning was lost.

Then it was copied in that form by other publications, and I felt violated. However, I pray that it could have brought comfort or inspiration to people anyway.

I offer the poem Limitations, hoping you too, will find it inspirational, and bring you a new appreciation of the beauty of the world God created.

Limitations

I cannot make the sun to rise,
however strong I'd be.
I cannot fill the sky with blue,
nor still a rolling sea!

I cannot make a rainbow,
nor wash the trees with rain.
I cannot make a bird to sing,
nor ripen fields of grain!

I cannot usher in the dawn,
nor warm the day at noon;
I cannot make the sun to set,
nor hang the amber moon!

I cannot light a firefly,
nor catch the early dew.
I cannot build a mountain
with peaks of purple hue!

I cannot measure up to that
which God would have me be;
But I can shout about His love!
He gave His Son for me!

God's world is filled with many things
that I could never do.
But I can build a bridge of love
to reach from me to you!

"I can do all things through Christ,
who strengthens me." Philippians 4:13

When I was age about 55, my children gave me a pair of cross country skis, and poles. I had yearned for that for years. when I was a child, my Dad had made me skis, by soaking narrow boards in water, and bending them over a barrel for the curved ends. I loved those skis, and traveled miles on them back and forth to and from the country school I attended.

My brothers and I used to make ski jumps, and even though I was kind of small and skinny, I used to dare to sail over those jumps too.

The tracks I left in the snow always fascinated me, seeing the path where I had been, and the herringbone pattern as I climbed hills.

Now, I really enjoyed those tracks. I would ski around our farm fences, along the lane by the woods, and enjoy looking at all the tracks made by small and large animals as they scurried out of my way.

There are few things more soothing to the soul than to shush along, gliding down slopes, seeing the white world in all it's morning loveliness, the sun reflecting off the pristine hills and valleys. I can always feel a special closeness to God on these mornings, and it seems to inspire poetry in me. I carry a pad and pen, and occasionally stop and jot down a few thoughts to elaborate on when I return to the house.

I stop and look back at the tracks behind me, and create a bit of poetry. The following one was born on a January morning as I savored the stillness on the hill.

January

A brand new year,
A brand new book,
Untouched pages
Like the untouched white
Of new fallen snow!

Lord, what can I write
on these pages of life ahead?
Help me to fill them with good things,
And leave a decent pattern
On the fresh, yet to be determined
Blank spaces!

Like foot prints on the
Soft, clean snow,
Let my mark upon the surface
Of the New Year
Tell those who come after me,
That I walked with Jesus!

"Whoever follows me will never walk in darkness, but will have the light of the world." John 8:12

Sharing the Son of God with others seems to be my purpose in life, and I seem compelled to do that in whatever I write.

January 6 is the designated day of Epiphany, and as I tried to think of ways to pass along this great gift of the Savior, this poem came to mind one cold, stormy January day as I sat by the window of my log house. Snug and warm, with a blaze in the fireplace, the storm raging outside, I looked forward to the smooth, inviting snow that would be visible when the storm had ceased.

It was then that I waited patiently for another ski morning. And my thoughts turned to the Epiphany of our Lord, when He sent the star to hover over Bethlehem to guide the wise men to find Him there in the manger in a stable, or cave, whichever it was.

We don't have to know for sure the exact situation of that long ago time. But we do know that God set a star in the sky for guidance and light.

And we know that He wants to use us as lights to shine a pathway for others to see and know His Son and our Savior, Jesus Christ.

Epiphany Star

Long ago, God used
The Epiphany star
To lead the wise men from afar
To find
The Christ Child.

In our day, God uses us
As stars
To lead others to know
The risen Christ!

Do we shine bright enough
To pierce the dark
Of the world
With our message of
Hope?

Does our light glow
Steadily enough
To guide other souls
To Christ?

Lord God,
Pour your light in
Our hearts
And let it overflow to make a path
That clearly leads
To you!

…"in which you shine like stars in the universe."
Philippians 2:15

MARCH

Did the groundhog see his shadow?
Will income tax go away?
Will Saint Patrick's Day turn
From green to gold?
Will the March winds
Blow away?

March is a month of
In between,
The last of winter, the
First of spring.
The only reliable part of March is,
We never know what it
Will bring!

An icy blizzard,
Or early thaw;
Whatever will be, will be;
I think God stuck march
In between
To give us variety!

But we know from the years
That have gone before,
March is a time to repent;
And we live through March
With joy, for we know,
That Easter comes after Lent!

FROM STORM TO SUN

One bitter blast of winter's rage
Before the birth of spring;
Sleet and snow and icy wind,
Grim weather's final fling!

We know It's only for a while,
And then the flowers will bloom.
The clouds will pass, the sun will shine
And sweep away the gloom!

I see a parallel of life,
The winter time of age.
The storms of life pile up on me,
A tempestuous last page!

And though I'm not quite ready yet
For time to take its' toll…
I'll not fear death, for then will be
The springtime of my soul!

"I will fear no evil, for thou are
With me." Psalm 23

The Turning Point

The old man sadly turned away, putting an arm around his wife's bowed shoulders.

Tears glistened on their cheeks as they slowly made their way home. Together, they turned for one last look at the three still forms, the crosses silhouetted against the gold of the evening sky.

At home, the grieving couple sat down to their humble evening meal, bowed their heads as the old man prayed in his trembling voice, "Father, bless this food you have given us." And with tears streaming down into his graying beard, he added, "And Lord, please have mercy on our son!"

In silence, the old couple sat, scarcely touching their food. Then the woman said, "But did you hear what the Christ said to our son?"

"When?"

"Just before the end."

"Yes, I heard." he answered, "He said, today you will be with me in Paradise."

"Well, we know that He was the Son of God. So then, don't you think that means that He is going to take our son with him to Heaven?"

"Yes, I believe so."

The old man looked up with new light in his sad eyes. "Isn't it strange; all of our lives we tried to be good parents, and tried to tell our son that living a Godly life would save his soul?"

"And isn't it strange that in our son's last moments he showed us that only faith in Jesus will save us?"

"Yes," the old woman agreed. "It isn't what we do that saves our souls, but it is what Jesus has already done for us!"

Each Easter Sunday...

I look into the past and see our small ones,
 Crisp and shiny in home sewn outfits
And polished shoes.
    I feel the excitement of this
      Blessed day as I see the sun come up
        Brighter than yesterday,
And I feel JOY.

I look back beyond those days and see
Another mother,
      Face upturned and filled with awe,
        Her grief of yesterday wiped clean away!
Today her battered Son is whole again
 And lives
For you, for me!

Because of this I look ahead
And see the day when Jesus comes
      To claim His own, His everyone.
For it is everyone He died to save,
And give to each the gift of life!
I weep for those of the everyone
      Who turn away and reject
        His timeless gift!

"But thanks be to God! He gives us
The victory through our Lord Jesus Christ."
1Corinthians 15:57

New Perspectives

The door is always open
and the welcome mat is out,
to the entrance of the Kingdom
when you turn your life about!

There is no high admission fee,
no difficult exam;
no rigid rules to follow,
I can come just as I am!

When you give your life to Jesus,
your thoughts and wishes shift,
from the things you thought you
Had to have,
to God's most precious Gift!

After that, your greatest need
is to share this joy with others.
With the world, your neighbors, and your
friends; with your sisters and your brothers!

Thinking about Mary

The older I grow, the more I cherish time spent with the grandchildren. They are all growing up so fast.

When I am privileged to be with Dustin for a while, I can't help looking ahead to what his life may include. I hope college, a good career, hopefully not going off to a future war, but the future for our children is so uncertain.

I know God has a plan for each one of them and we pray that they will learn what that plan is.

When I'm with Dustin, I can't help thinking deep thoughts, about Mary, the mother of Jesus. The Lutheran church always put most of the emphases on Jesus, not Mary. We do honor her and love her, but I don't think we give her as prominent a spot as our Catholic sisters and brothers do.

But when I look at Dustin, and hug him and love him, I think of what it must have been like for Mary, as she looked on her little boy, Jesus and hugged Him, and loved Him, all the while knowing (and I'm convinced she did know) the horrible ordeal He would endure when He was grown.

It is so painful for us when any of our children or grandchildren are sad, or have problems, or when we are concerned for their physical welfare. (Like mothers of young people going off to war). Just think of the anguish Mary experienced during Jesus' growing up years.

There was nothing Mary could do to stop it happening, it was ordained, and all for us human people, to pay our way to Heaven when we die. And Mary wouldn't have stopped it if she could, because she trusted the Lord and was completely obedient.

So, when you hug your little boy (or girl), think about Mary, and be grateful to her for being willing to give birth to our Savior, Jesus, and to suffer the agony of losing him to a cruel mob. A mob, whom Jesus forgave for crucifying him.

The greatest thing ever for us to be thankful for.

Mother's Day in Bethlehem

So many, many years ago
A Mother watched her son;
As He played just like the other boys,
Laughing and having fun.

I wonder what that Mother felt,
Knowing what she knew:
That her Son would suffer horribly,
And die for you and you and you.

The pain she must have felt that day,
As He hung upon the cross,
Had to be greater than the pain we feel
No matter what our loss!

Mothers down through the ages
Still suffer for their own;
But we know they are really God's children,
Only given to us on loan.

Just like Mary of Bethlehem,
We have to let them go;
And trust in God to keep them safe,
We just love them and tell them so!

Choices, While Growing Old

Sometimes I think that this age, "old", is the best one yet. If I choose to make it so.

Right now, I have many choices. I can come and go as I please. I can fix myself a decent meal, or I can make myself a peanut butter sandwich.

If I choose, I can sit down and read a book, or I can spend some time on the computer, either researching something, or simply playing solitaire.

If I choose, I can meet one of my children for lunch, or I can do some volunteer work. Or I can offer to do some dishwashing or clothes folding for the busy children in my life.

I do realize that all of this could change overnight (and probably will) if I become disabled and cannot take care of myself, if this would prevent me from maintaining my little log home and my car.

But mostly, right now, choices are mine. If I choose to dwell on all that has been lost in my life, then I would just dissolve into a sea of tears and be of no use to anyone.

If I choose to yearn to turn back the clock to a time when Husband was living and my children were all small and close, then I would have no peace in the years I have left.

If I choose to let all the frustrations of my physical limitations overwhelm me, then I would find no pleasure in the things I am able to do.

If I choose to complain constantly about my painful arthritis and my overweight, then I would have no compassion to sympathize with the pain and suffering of others.

If I choose to moan and groan each time I look in the mirror and see my white hair and wrinkled face, then I would have no smiles and laughter to share with other people.

If I choose to look on the downside of every bad situation, depressing myself and everyone around me, then I wouldn't be able to stand my own company, and neither would anyone else.

Growing old is not for sissies!

But I believe that being able to face an uncertain and limited future (at this age it is limited), with some measure of peace and happiness, is not possible without the continuing faithful support of a loving God. Instead, always remembering to thank Him for all the good things in my life (past and present), how He has walked beside me in joys and sorrows, and will walk with me in the present and on into Eternity.

Lord, help me to make good choices with whatever time I have left.

God's House Cleaning

When guests are coming to my home,
I like to have it neat.
I like to scrub and polish,
and bake some yummy treat.

I throw away the litter
that piled up through the week.
I clean the hearth and lay a fire,
wash windows 'til they squeak.

When Jesus comes to live with me,
inside my head and heart;
I need to clean the corners
to make sure He won't depart.

I need to throw away a lot
of things that make Him sad;
the selfishness and gossip,
some evil thoughts I've had.

But I realize I cannot clean
this dingy house of mine
to make it 'good enough' for Him.
I'm human, He's divine!

I am so very grateful
that He comes in anyway,
and covers up the mess in here,
and promises to stay!

Now that's God's whole idea,
that by His sacrifice,
Christ covered all the sin in me,
when He paid the ultimate price!

"Wash me and I will be whiter than snow."
Psalm 51:7

Moments of Gladness

Let me be glad for THIS moment, Lord!
The road is smooth and wide,
The mist hangs low on the distant hills,
Shrouding trees on either side.

The windshield wipers are singing a song,
As they splash the rain away!
The mist is rising, the sun shines through;
A rainbow is on the way!

Let me rejoice in THIS moment, Lord,
For this grandchild asleep on my arm,
These moments won't last, too soon will be past,
Precious memories to keep me warm!

Let me be glad for THIS moment, Lord,
As I walk out the road with Bailey.
I'm glad to be able to take each step,
And I thank you, Lord, for it daily!

Let me be glad for EACH moment, Lord,
Whether rain or storms cloud my way.
I know that the sun will eventually shine
Bringing light to the gloomiest day!

Let me be glad for the SUN, Lord;
A gift that's so warm and free!
But gladder still, for YOUR SON, Lord,
Who has opened Heavens doors for me!

"I will be glad and rejoice in your love."
Psalm 31:7

"God on Hold?"

Sometimes we tend to put God 'on hold';
    With a plan to return to Him when we are old.
    But life goes so fast, this chance might not last,
And who knows what our future could hold?

Sometimes we live as though He's not here,
    We take all the credit when good days appear.
    We go on our merry old way, often neglecting
    Even to pray.
He keeps right on calling, but we just don't hear!

He showers us daily with gifts here on earth,
    Our families, our homes, the miracle of birth.
    The food that we eat, the clothes that we wear.'
    We take, without even being aware
That God is the giver of all we are worth!

Some day we'll awaken and look on His face,
    And realize God loves the whole human race.
    We need Him, all of us, young ones and old.
    And how blessed we are that
God doesn't put us on hold!

"For we are God's fellow workers."
1 Corinthians 3:9

Old Barn Memories

I learned that the barn next door, the one that used to be ours when we farmed, is going to be torn down. For a moment I felt bad, but not for long. I'd rather see it torn down that to see it rot away and fall down from old age, like we see so many end up.

The process has started, with the side boards removed. It stands there like a pitiful skeleton, waiting it's demise.

It's funny, the memories that come back, thinking about that old barn and the past. All the summers of filling it's lofts with hay. Loose hay, when we first began farming. We used an old 'hay loader', that was pulled behind the wagon, which was pulled by the tractor.

One person had to drive the tractor, and one had to stand on the wagon and pitch the forkfuls of hay toward the front and gradually pile it up until the load passed the wooden "standard." The standard was a part of the front of the rack, where you would stand and drive horses in the days when horses were used. We had horses, but we never did use them to load hay.

In those olden days, the load was backed into the hay barn alley, and the 'hay fork' was lowered to unload with. That consisted of two big "fork things" that lived at the top of the barn ceiling until haying time. These two big fork things would be pushed down into the load to hold a big lump of hay.

Then the tractor was driven, pulling some ropes that hoisted the big clump of hay up to the ceiling. Then someone had to trip the rope that swung the whole thing to the side of the mow, tripped again to release the clump of hay onto the mow. Over and over, until the wagon was empty.

When the baler came into existence, we did have an elevator and put the bales on it, which carried them up to the loft, where people had to stack them. What a hot, sticky, itchy job that was. In my younger days, I too, used to walk up that long, long elevator to get to the mow.

That old barn was a lot like our old dining room table, being the scene of many a discussion. Husband and I would untangle a lot of 'kid' problems as we did the chores. And I guess the kids used to untangle a lot of "parent" problems while they did theirs too.

Before I got so old, I used to do the "schottische" down the walk after spreading it with barn lime. I do also remember Husband looking at me as I did that like I had really gone over the edge this time. He never did schottisch. I can't even remember how that dance step went. I must have been a lot lighter then too.

Some things that happened in that barn were funny and some not so funny. When daughter Sandy was little, she used to sit on the edge of one of the calf pens and watch her dad milk. Once she fell into the calf pen and was covered with the gooey green stuff.

When son Bruce was five years old, and always wanting to help do the 'big men's' chores, he was pushing a bale of hay down the chute, and fell through it an broke his elbow. We had to drive and drive to find a doctor home that time of evening.

And in that barn, when I carried the milk from the barn to the milk house, that is where a lot of my poetry was born. On the white filter disc, between pails of milk.

That barn had many uses, besides housing cows. Upstairs, one section was used to house capons, like a thousand of them, and one year that section housed pigs.the year we had pigs in there, a water pipe burst, flooding that pig pen, and ran down into the milking part, filling the gutters and overflowing them.

Husband had just had surgery, and I was about seven months pregnant. Very foolishly I tried to shovel the water out of the gutters, until a couple of older neighbor men came and helped. Uff-Da!

Early on we had work horses in horse stalls, two goats lived there, and in the rear of the barn stalls were built for riding horses.

And of course, hundreds of cats lived and died there; and swallows built their nests right over head where we milked the cows.

As the barn aged, right along with Husband and myself, the windows began to sag, and every fall it was necessary to cover them with plastic. What a disgusting job that was, and it was my job to do it, until later years when Sonia did it. The plastic was held on with boards and nailed into the barn boards, and I guess it did help to keep out the cold winter winds.

Now that I know it's going down, I walk in there once in a while, and my mind goes back, dragging out memories buried in the past, only to bring s huge lump in my throat and a few tears, (actually a lot).

I hear the echoes of scenes and sounds long forgotten, and I feel "Husband's" presence keenly.

Like the old 'topless' silo. When it was time to "open" the silo and begin feeding silage to the cows. We would shovel it out with a wide silage fork and then carry big shovels full to each cow in the stanchions.

30

One of these "ladies" was such a hog! She would save her own pile and reach as far as she could in both ways to eat as much as she could of the cow next to her. She wouldn't touch hers until their was all gone.

On the wall where the telephone used to hang are the evidences of long ago transactions; telephone numbers for the feed mill, the artificial inseminator, children's phone numbers, many in Husband handwriting. And some in mine, accompanied by pictures doodled while I talked on the phone.

The little square box where the radio used to blare out "Good morning, good morning, I'm glad to be on hand, good morning, good morning to you" by Boone and Erickson. (Only you seniors will remember them).

Today the burial took place. I am surprised how much it bothered me. Great-grandson Austin and I went to look at them digging the hole, and it reminded me on an enormous grave. And the next time we went to look, the barn was gone. The scene looked so desolate with out that old red barn standing there.

I had a sick, empty feeling inside, since over half of my life time was buried in that grave. Maybe I'll get used to the emptiness each time I drive by it.

But lighten up, Old Cow Belle, leave the past in the past. Enjoy all the good things in your life, and be thankful for them.

Peace

Leave the past in the past;
Bury your pain and your sorrow.
Be glad for the good things today,
And look for a brighter tomorrow!

The days of the past are behind you,
Never to come back again,
Just look with hope to the future;
Don't look back to see where you've been.

The peace that you need comes from Jesus;
He will stay by your side every day.
So give Him you pain and your sorrow,
And you heartache will soon go away!

Leave the past in the past,
Let Jesus heal all your sorrows.
Invite Him to live in your heart every day,
And you will have brighter tomorrows!

…"And by His wounds we are healed."
Isaiah 53:5

God's Voice

God speaks to me in the morning,
in the glow of the rising sun.
In the hush of the world,
the song of a bird
announcing the day has begun.

God speaks to me at the noontime,
when half of the day is past.
Have I followed His lead?
Have I planted one seed?
Have I done one thing
that will last?

God speaks to me in the midnight,
when cares and worries draw near.
"Dear child" He whispers,
"lean forever on me";
then I slumber in peace
without fear.

God speaks to us if we listen,
for He loves each person the same.
His Son died for you and for me and for all!
Just believe on His
wonderful name!

"My sheep listen to my voice."
John 10:27

September, for Mary

September sings a glad song,
Blue skies and crimson hills,
Of goldenrod and milkweed pods...
And sumac's scarlet frills.

September brings out children
a-laughing off to school,
With bikes and books and knapsacks;
And teachers' faithful rule.

September brings the memories
That suddenly come back....
Of children grown, and loved ones gone,
Love letters in a pack.

September brings the cool nights
With firelights a-glow,
And friends and family growing close
Where love and friendships flow.

September, Oh September!
I think I love you best.
I see God's hand more clearly
This month than all the rest!

Sanctuary

Oh, God! Reach down with soothing touch
And calm the troubling winds that blow into
My world.

As each day dawns and starts anew, I pray
My stupidity will be a little less, and all I long to
Be, come forth. To say some word to those I love…
To heal a hurt or ease a pain…or simply understand.

If I could only stop my tongue when words
Do nothing good; or keep my house all neat and clean, and mend the socks
and all those mundane things. But…

My mind and soul go soaring high, the socks forgotten while I take my
pen, and wasting time, just for a while, I daydream…about my
family…about God…noble things I'll never do.

In the end my pen is idle too, and nothing on the page appears…and all
the lovely thoughts I've had
Have flown away.

Shrugging the wispy daydreams from my mind, I run to catch the hours
I've used, confident anyway that God has heard. That He knows my
wretched nothingness, and even knowing, loves.

"Be still and know that I am God."
Psalm 46:9

Something from Nothing

LORD....
I'm a worthless blob of clay today!
Can't seem to focus or find my way.
Please throw me on your turning wheel,
And shape me with your Holy zeal
So my life will make some sense today!

LORD...
Place your gentle hands on me,
And mold me to what you want me to be.
Just smooth away the wretched bumps
And eliminate uneven humps.
To make some worthwhile thing of me.

LORD POTTER....
Use this useless clay,
To make a vessel of me anyway,
With inside large enough to hold
Whatever will make me strong and bold,
To share the Good News every day!

BUT LORD...
Just knowing that you care,
And walk beside me everywhere
To show the way that I should go,
I'm grateful that you love me so!
Please help me now, your love to share!

Isaiah 64:8, "O Lord, You are
the Potter, we are the clay. We are the
work of your hands."

Happiness

The only way to be truly happy is to BE TRULY HAPPY!

You are thinking, *"What does she know? Maybe her situation is far different from mine! Maybe she has good health, a good income, nice home, no financial worries. Anyone can be happy in a situation like that!"*

Wrong! Happiness does not depend on outward trappings. Happiness begins with opening your heart's door and inviting Jesus to come in and live there.

I think I am kind of a happy old person. And situations are relative. Some people, if they really knew mine, would throw up their hands and wonder how I can survive as I do, let alone be happy about it.

And some, like those in third world countries would envy my apparent good fortune.

I believe that happiness begins with an attitude of gratitude. I am grateful to have a roof over my head, and pray that my questionable health will permit me to live in my house until I "kick off ."

Once a long time ago, I was admonished 'in a letter to the editor, about being so *eternally grateful!* Sorry, I can't help it. But for the grace of God, I too, could be living in a mud hut somewhere in Africa. So I am grateful that I don't.

I am grateful that my social security check covers my expenses. I am grateful for my children's concern. I am grateful that they have taken over my lawn mowing. I am grateful that they care about me and each other.

Lest you think I'm a self-righteous old lady, I am not so happy when I find a leak in some water pipe, or the dog throws up on the floor, or a skunk wanders by and sprays his perfume nearby, or I bake a batch of whole wheat bread and it doesn't raise, and I have to feed it to the birds!!

But those are minor things. Some really big things, like Husband's death, do take away all happiness for a while. But nothing can take away the security of knowing that God is always near, giving His strength when I have none of my own. I'm learning as I age, that this little "trip," from birth to death, goes by so fast.

And, all the unfortunate things that happen to you, are only as bad as your reaction to them.

SO BE HAPPY!!

Weaver's Prayer

O God, I humbly ask of you
To daily weave yourself into
The fabric of my life!
That knots and snarls and broken thread
Will not deter the work ahead,
But strengthen me for strife!

This garment I am weaving, Lord,
I pray will be with your accord,
And pleasing in your sight.
I'll use the pattern sent by you
And try to weave as He would do,
And follow in His light!

The skeins I choose I wish to be
A witness bold for all to see
How great is Jesus' love!
I'll ask for strength from you, O Lord;
And find direction in your word
You spoke from Heaven above!

And though I diligently weave
My whole life through, I know I'll leave
Undone what I should do.
But through Christ's blood some day I'll shed
This mortal shroud, and wear instead
A gown of righteousness,
That you have fashioned just for me
To wear in Heaven, eternally!

October Sky

When God created color
He knew we'd all love blue!
So he spread the great dome overhead
With that brilliant, sparkling hue!

And though the sky is always blue,
It changes every day,
Sometimes it' s filled with cotton clouds,
Or overcast with gray.

The mornings find it edged in pink,
Backed up with golden rays;
And in our valley, mists arise
To greet October days.

In all the months, of all the years
The sky's forever blue.
But somehow for October,
God made a "bluer" blue!

…"And God called the expanse sky"
Genesis 1:6

The Weathered Old House

The old house stands at the top of the hill,
sad, and weathered and gray.
It seems to be scanning the valley below
and the distant hills far, far away.

I feel that house has a heart and a soul,
and a song, even though it is old.
I feel that it's thinking of days long ago,
When a family these walls did enfold.

I hear children playing around the front door,
While Mother is cooking inside,
And soon up that long, long driveway will come
the Father, his arms open wide.

The supper is ended, the dishes are done,
the children all washed and in bed,
and Mother sits down by the side of each one,
and stays 'til the prayers have been said.

And so the old house is re- living again
the days of the long, long ago,
It's kind of like me, looking back on my life,
and how swiftly those years seemed to go!

The gray of my hair, and my weathered old face,
are the clues that my life has been long.
But like that old house at the top of the hill,
I'm facing each day with a song!

Thank God for Little Things

For giving me children to brighten my days,
The bonus of grandchildren, blessings always;
For a cup of hot coffee,
And work to do,
For songs on the radio all the day through!

For the sun coming up, it's warmth at noon,
For soft evening shadows, the silvery moon.
The green of the grass, the blue of the sky;
For whispering breezes, the birds that fly!

For food to eat, and something to wear,
For strength from the Lord for crosses we bear.
For freedom to worship however we choose,
For our church, our pastor, who tells
The Good News!

Reading over my list, I have to agree,
None of these blessings are 'little' to me!
Each one is a gift from our
Father above,
Because of His generous, wonderful
Love!

"Give thanks in all circumstances."
1 Thessalonians 5:18

Growing Angels and Raising Sea Monkeys

I am a sucker for the 'unconventional', and so it is no surprise when I spotted the "Grow an Angel" packet on the counter of the dollar store. I just *had* to take one home.

The instructions said to "put this little angel in a pan of lukewarm water, and watch her grow to twice her size. So I did, knowing that the grandchildren would also get a kick out of it.

And it did! Grow to twice it's size! Then we took it out of the water, and let it shrink back again. And then we put it in the water again, and it grew again. The grandchildren checked it out each morning to see if it has changed. I don't know how many times it will change, but as of now, she is still growing and shrinking.

The Sea Monkey thing, was also an unconventional that I couldn't resist. This happened a long time ago when some other grandchildren were of the age to be inquisitive, just like Grandma.

That packet too, was spotted on the counter of a dime store. (At that time there really was a dime store.) Those directions said, "Grow live Sea Monkeys. Watch them come alive before your very eyes."

I fell for it, and with tongue in cheek, took one home. The directions said to fill a small jar with tepid water, and pour in the packet of monkey food. So I did. Then it said to add the packet of "monkey seeds" and let it sit for a day or two. I did, thinking, "sure, there will be monkeys here tomorrow."

And guess what! The next day there were little black dots sailing around in the water. The next day these little black dots had grown to be little round things with two little dots like eyes. The Grandchildren came each day to see what had happened.

Then….little ruffly things grew around those little heads and a small transparent body appeared next. They dashed around in the jar like mad. They multiplied like rabbits; and soon the jar was filled with the squirmy, repulsive little creatures. They reminded me of maggots!

I asked the grandchildren if they wanted to take the jar full home. But the Mom said, "No thanks!"

So I watched them squirm around for a couple of days, and they grew more and more repulsive, so I finally flushed them down the toilet stool.

So much for raising exotic things!

Sometimes and Sometimes

Sometimes our lives are filled with joy,
The sun shines bright all day!
We give our thanks to God above,
For His help along our way.

Sometimes our lives are filled with cares,
The clouds hang dark and low.
Our feeble frame betrays us again,
Our steps are faltered and slow.

We cry to God to "fix us up!"
To take away our pain,
To heal our ills and soothe our cares,
And show us the sunshine again!

But…our greatest Sometime will come one day,
When our life on earth is through;
No pain, no sadness, no cares at all,
Because Jesus died for you, and me too.

Sunday Morning

The house is still, no voices heard
As I rise and prepare for the day.
I think of the Sunday mornings
That the years have stolen away.

The children all clean and polished,
And Husband fresh-shaven and neat;
The voices of family discussions,
Some joking and some not too sweet!

Together we all went to worship,
Not a choice, just something we do;
And now looking back, I'm glad that
We did.
There was peace and love in that pew!

The children have grown and have families,
And they too, spend time in a pew.
They grew in their faith in our Savior,
So their children know Jesus too.

I sit by my table this morning,
The dog with her head on my feet.
It's quiet and peaceful and pleasant,
But oh, how those memories repeat!

I really don't mind the alone-ness,
Things change as the years come and
Go.
But sometimes I long for the noises
Of Sunday mornings long, long ago!

The Wonders of Christmas

So long ago in Bethlehem
A baby boy was born.
From Heavenly realms He came to us
In that stable so forlorn.

I wonder if the night was cold,
And was there wind and snow?
Who stayed to tend the sheep
When the shepherds chose to go?

Above the clouds the angels' song
Echoed through the deep!
And did the stabled creatures keep
The little Babe from sleep?

It was such a humble setting
For the birthday of the Lord!
But in His way, He let us know
He came for all the world.

I wonder, do the children know
It's why we celebrate?
If they only know of Santa,
Please tell them now, don't wait!

And let them know their greatest gift
Is not beneath the tree....
It's Jesus' love within their hearts,
A gift to share, that's free!

"He sent His one and only Son into the
World that we might live through Him."
1 John 4:9

December Thanksgiving

There are always gifts and parties,
There's always mistletoe!
There are always bells a'ringing,
And sunshine on the snow!

There are always window shoppers
That gaze at wonderlands;
There are always hugs and laughter,
And lovers holding hands!

But high above the tumult,
If you listen with your heart,
You'll hear the angels singing
Their "Good News" to impart!

That God has sent the Savior,
To be born a little child,
In a chilly hillside stable
To a virgin sweet and mild!

This child will grow and teach, then die
And rise to set us free!
So we thank and praise His holy name,
As we trim our Christmas tree!

"For to us a child is born, to us a Son is
Given." Isaiah 9:6

Be Still...and Know

The Christmas rush is upon us now,
Thanksgiving day is past.
The "Big day" is drawing nearer,
The time goes by so fast!

Oh dear, we need to "do" so much,
Be ready before it's too late.
But the Advent days that have just begun
Are saying, instead, to "Wait."

To wait in wonder, for Jesus' birth;
The Savior of everyone.
Let's light a candle each day 'til then,
For the coming of the Son!

We'll bake our cookies and plan our gifts,
We'll laugh and enjoy each day.
We'll kiss our children and let them know
That we still will take time to play.

Let's pause in this hectic commercial time
To look past the glitter and glow,
To see Jesus the Babe in the manger,
From whom all blessings flow!

Remembering

Christmas is remembering
When the children all were small;
The laughter bouncing off the walls
To echo down the halls.

The whole gang trouping off to church
To hear the Glad Good News;
To see the candles glowing,
As they're lighted down the pews.

The meal prepared, the presents shared,
The Christmas story read,
The quiet late night moments
When the rest have gone to bed.

Christmas is remembering
The dear ones gone ahead,
The ones who now are spending it
With Jesus Christ, instead!

Dear Jesus, thank you for this day,
As we celebrate your birth.
The day you were born to save us,
Coming down from Heaven to Earth.

The Golden Years

Our early days were filled with stress,
But warm and full of happiness,
The children small, our work to do,
No time to whine or fret or stew!

Time races on, the children leave
We must slow down, we do believe.
Instead, we work, and work some more
For daily bread, and some to store.

And now at last, we're growing old,
We stop the race to enjoy the gold!
Alas, or feeble frames break down,
We spend our days in a hospital gown!

Our "Golden Years" are not so bright,
We've chased the rainbows out of sight!
Self pity doesn't help at all,
So dry the tears, get on the ball!

Believe that God is close beside,
The path before us smooth and wide.
The sky is blue, the sun is bright,
And He will make it turn out right!

Whatever comes, the good, the bad,
Look back on all the joys we've had!
Be glad we have our loved ones near,
God's hand on ours, no need to fear!

"Thy rod and thy staff, they comfort me."
Psalm 23

The Ups and Downs

The skies are low
And somber gray.
They wrap themselves around
my heart.
And only God, with loving hand
Can rend that gloomy
Veil apart.

These lower times
That I endure,
Can cause my heart
To cry with pain.
Then healing comes (from God alone)
Like glowing sunshine after rain!

I think I need these plunging depths,
So I can see
The glorious peaks
Of love and joy that
Flow to me....
The peace that comes when
Jesus speaks!

"I will turn their mourning into gladness"
Jeremiah 31:13

Losing Your Life's Mate

I know it's true that when you lose your life's mate, you will always carry them in your heart.

But I must also carry Husband in my head. It shows up in many ways. I always fill the car with the same kind of gas he did. I buy the same brand of pineapple he liked. I make beans the way he liked them. And chili.

But…if I find myself buying and eating raisins (which I hate) then I'll know I have a screw loose!

* * *

The older I grow, the more I realize what a short journey we travel on this earth!

In youth, time seems endless, the future stretches into infinity. In middle age, we get so caught up in the "busyiness" of life that the future still seems eons away.

Now, in my later years, I can see clearer. Even if old age should bring all sorts of woes, the future looks promising. My journey has been a good trip, with unspeakable joys and unspeakable sorrows, but now near life's end, I find that there will be a whole new world to discover. That THIS isn't all there is.

And all because Jesus died to make us God's children and inheritors of Eternal Life!

Visions

My entire family, my old family, all beat me to Heaven, and I like to wonder about what they might be doing there.

I think my Dad may have been growing fruit trees in God's orchards all these years, since 1968. I can see him grafting branches of different kinds onto trees to see what kinds of fruit it will produce. (Like he did here in his earthly orchard).

He must have quite a lot to show for it in the 26 years he worked on it before Mom joined him.

I can see Mom, standing on the edge of Heaven, bending down and dipping a silver brush into a pot of sparkling golden paint, creating the spectacular sunsets on the western horizons, that we enjoy each clear day.

My older brother Harvey, breathing easily, is most likely vigorously finishing a beautiful table for the Lord; made from some exotic wood, the top so smooth and shiny that it reflects the glory of the Lord. Almost like a mirror.

I see my brother Bob, at the edge of a ball field, surrounded by dozens of small boys, coaching them how to play fair; and rejoicing in either winning or losing. As he motions to some small boy, I see his hand, where a finger was severed on board his ship the U.S.S. Moose during a typhoon during WWII….is whole again!

And Husband. I can see him, whole and healthy, no heart trouble, no diabetes, no asthma…leading a golden caravan of snow mobilers, winding around and around the switchbacks, ever higher and higher climbing the sparkling white mountains of Eternity. What a lovely vision to carry in my heart

The New Year

What will the new year hold? You ask,
Laughter, or tears and sorrow?
Be glad if you can, try not to be sad…
Don't dwell on the woes of tomorrow!

Don't yearn toward the future, don't dwell in the past.
Try being content with today.
The past is behind, tomorrow's not ours.
Just follow, let God lead the way.

"…My grace is sufficient for you."
2nd Corinthians:9

One Day Closer

When the sun goes down
At the end of the day
And the light in the sky grows dim;
I think of the hours now lost to me,
But I'm one day closer to Jesus, my Lord,
One day closer to Him!

I'll try not to dwell on the days gone by,
And the things I neglected to do.
For the past is behind me, I can't bring it back;
But I can start each morning anew,
Bringing me one day closer to seeing my Lord,
One day closer to Him!

Now that another birthday is past,
And a new year for me will begin;
I can go forward with hope in my heart
Because I'm a
WHOLE YEAR
Closer to Him!

Printed in the United States
45848LVS00006B/150